Silhouettes of Self-Doubt

and the Fires We Let Burn

A collection of poetry

Miranda Mohr

India | USA | UK

Made with ❤ on the BookLeaf Publishing Platform
www.bookleafpub.in
www.bookleafpub.com

Dedication

This book is dedicated to my three angels in heaven: my daughters Ava and Caroline, and my mother Judith, as well as to the little girl I never got to be.

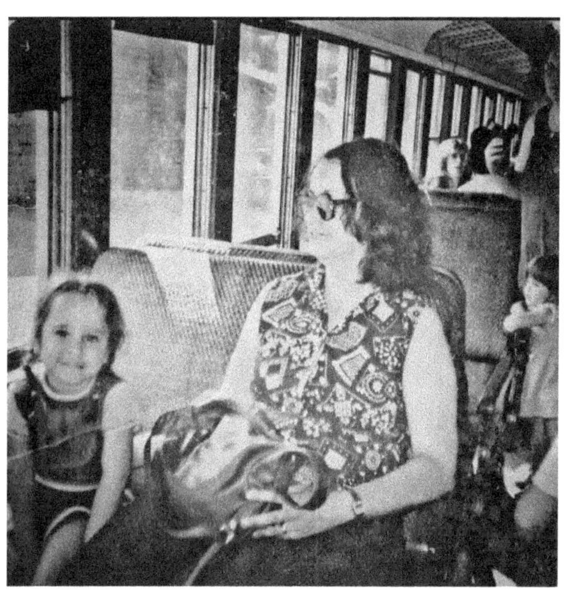

Acknowledgement

I want to say thank you to everyone who has supported and encouraged me to continue writing. You know who you are. But especially to my amazing husband, James.

Preface

Poetry has helped me unlock my emotions since I was a teenager, no matter what I went through. This book emerged from my love of the art of writing meaningful words and my desire to share what normal feelings can look like. For me, even the dark emotions have purpose, and it is when you can see the big picture that you are truly alive. This book is decades in the making.

Contents

PART ONE

The Darkness In Grief

Life

A rose with its petals
Sits in a vase,
Sagging over the side.
A single petal falls.
No one mourns,
But the rose itself.
Without each pedal,
The rose itself is lost.
The petals together
Are its life.
Every dying petal
Takes some life away.
The rose crumbles,
With sadness and tears.
As the last petal falls,
And its purpose
Is gone.

Unanswered Questions

In my eyes, you were a bright light,
Until I witnessed the abuse.
My mama's terror, quite apparent,
I tried to imagine a cause.
What could she have done to deserve
Punishment surpassing a child's?
As I understood the severity,
Each cry made me want to hate you more.
When your anger turned on your child,
It made me feel insignificant
I thought the rage was somehow my fault—
That I was unworthy of your love.
Your actions proved intolerable.
We left you to live your dismal life.
Your letters could not deter our disgust,
So silence prevailed over concern.
Disregard made me question why
I could deserve such horridness.
A shocking end to an unhappy life—
I didn't have enough time to ask.
I never understood you back then.
The chance to even try was taken.
My love, consumed by fury and anguish,
A permanent affliction to my heart.

That Morning

I woke that morning from the deepest of sleep,
Worn down by the weight of baby number two in the
house.
Finally, a calm sleep, free of worry or fear—
A good motivation came with me as I woke him.
His hungry little eyes gleaming,
Eager to wake his grandma and play,
Ready to leap onto her bed and give her kisses.
We walked in, without real knowledge of what lay
ahead,
As your grandson spoke to you happily,
Oblivious to your stillness, your silence.
I realized there was a thickness in the air,
And my throat immediately choked up.
I couldn't look at you for a long time,
Though every bone in my body already knew.
He still spoke to you a while in his babble,
As if having a conversation with himself.
Your granddaughter finally woke in her crib
And let out a cry full of her temper.
At that moment, I could wait no longer,
And I looked at your wide, placid eyes.
Eyes that offered no peace, just turmoil.
My heart raged with the same temper.
"Mommy, no," is all I could squeeze out,
And its repetition made my feelings stop.
The tears halted as quickly as they came, like a
rotated valve,
And I headed straight for problem-solving mode.
I shook, I yelled, I felt for your heart to beat.
The coldness shocked me, and a single fat tear fell.
The sound of sirens are embossed in my head,
Along with your last expression, so much like mine.
I will never fully move on from that morning.
A lot of strange people in and out of your house,

Many "how are you's" and a great deal of staring
later,
I am still left with the same question:
The what-ifs that come with death.

Seven Year Silence

(Ode to Mommy)

My silence speaks to me sometimes,
Bringing me memories from when you were here.
Unbelievable, implausible,
Inconceivable, staggering.
How can it all be gone?
The maternal bond ceased,
Seven years without you.
I thought you would be there,
Forever and infinite,
Always, without end.
You were meant to teach me
What's wrong, what's right.
Come, please, I'm calling.
Anger at the neglect of your answer—
A picture falls. A light flickers.
What does it mean? Is it you? You visit me in
dreams,
And you talk to me the whole way through,
But I cannot understand a word.
And I wake more confused than before.

How can it be seven years without you?
No scolding or soothing,
No crying or yelling,
No joy or peace.
I know you tried to stay.
I know you had to go.
But the pain rips through me,
Day after day.
Come, please, I'm falling,
All alone, I shred away.
They tell me to accept it,
To move on, like that is possible.
"Use the positive to negate the negative"—
Words easier spoken than lived.
My tears, meant to wash away the years,
Have only brought misery without ease.
They say that I have a problem with my heart,
I say it's shattered into a thousand pieces.
My silence speaks to me sometimes,
Bringing me memories from when you were near.

A Bond Permanently Severed

I feel like a tremendous weight is ever-present.
It is the grievous wound left from your passing.
Picture a huge chunk of my heart being ripped out,
With a warning that was never really taken seriously.
I cannot imagine my life without you, and yet here it
is.
Eight years have come and gone in a flash.
A grave to visit is not enough for me to fill the gap.
It is a life-altering loss I will never recover from.
I try to remember the memories and move forward,
But I am not strong enough to file the pain away.
Like when I was a young girl, we used to wake
And make Dad's coffee together In the morning.
You gave me my care and understanding.
You gave me my fight and demand for respect.
My laughter, my sarcasm, and my love of life.
My belief that I could be a good person at all.
You made Dad leave when things were atrocious,
And went through agony moving on from that.
But even when the times were hard and things went
wrong,

You would always say, "It will be okay," and that was
enough.
I feel deep remorse for how I treated you.
When your own mother died, I was too selfish to be
there.
I can hear you in my head now, saying, "It's okay."
But just because I was young doesn't forgive it.
You even supported me when I wanted to write.
Even though I wasn't good, you encouraged me
anyway.
And you inspire me now, even in death.
Writing is the only way I keep my sanity.
I love you as I did when I was a little girl,
Deeply and with the purest dedication.
Holding your hand so I wouldn't run away,
Back when I was untouched by the heavy loss and
pain in this world.
I miss talking with you about my latest screw-ups,
Shaking your head at me, you would always calm
me.
And you realized when I was being too stubborn
To accept the help or advice from you.
No one in this world knows me as you knew me,
From the inside out and everything in between.
It is a bond permanently severed from its roots,
Never to grow anew and bloom great flowers.
Even now I cannot let myself feel the pain.
If I do, I will collapse and struggle to be the same.

Your Last Picture

Thirteen short years ago,
My heart had a sudden seizure.
It cracked and broke all at once,
And it has never been the same.
The battle you waged was lost,
And you were gone forever.
A warm, beautiful woman
Taken too soon from this world.
Months before, against your wishes,
I took a random picture:
You and your fourth grandson,
While he danced for you with glee.
It was Christmas morning,
Pajamas were the dress code,
Presents had to be opened,
And you two were being silly.
How was I to know at the time
That would be your last picture?
I couldn't understand then
How much I would look at it later.
To see you in mid-treatment,
Your hand covering the baldness,
Your body diminished to half its size,
Your features pale and withdrawn.
But I can also see your joy
In the little boy in front of you.
We loved him fiercely together.
You spoiled him as a Grammy should.
And I can see the ample tree,
Varied ornaments and garland,
Many we had since I was small,
Staples during Christmas time.
And after this picture was taken,
We laughed and cried together often.
The highs of my life as it was starting,
The lows of your life as it was ending.

And then your granddaughter arrived,
And you were away, "getting better."
"Nothing but up from the bottom",
I had no idea what the bottom would actually be.
I thought I had more time with you,
To let you smother me with love,
To argue with you about nothing,
To watch you relish being a grandmother.
Then we were all home on Seymour Terrace,
Spending our last moments together.
I know now you came home to meet her,
And to show us your love until the end.
I still hear your voice so clearly—
When happiness is holding me,
And when pain has brought me to tears:
"We will get through it together."
I will never be alone,
Because you are ever part of me.
As I age, I see more of you
In myself and your grandchildren.
And when I miss you so terribly,
And the wound begins to reopen,
I think of the strong woman who raised me,
My loving mommy, who you will always be.

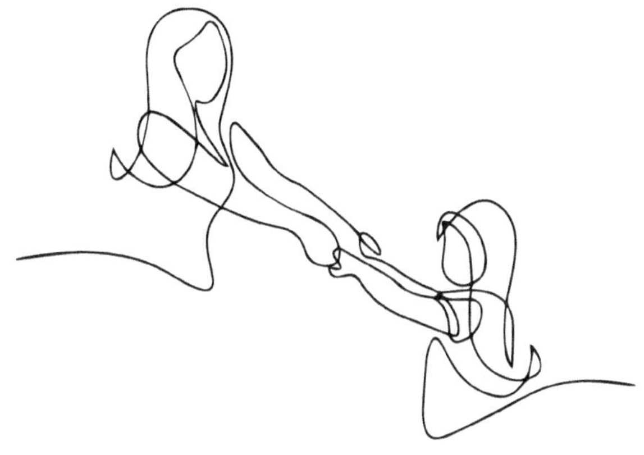

Mother

You gave so much to everyone,
Sometimes you forgot about yourself.
There is so much more you wanted,
So many more you could have helped.
But as you pass on, Mother,
We hope that you are at peace.
A part of us will always be with you,
You'll be missed forever, to say the least.

Saturated Loneliness

I feel like I am coming apart internally,
Like my seams are coming undone from underneath.
I am suffocating in sorrow-filled memories,
Drowning in a fear-filled tub I crafted for myself.
It feels too late to exit from this path I have chosen;
I've lost sight of where it ends or begins.
I am too far out into the vast, relentless ocean,
I cannot see the shore anymore.
My dreams are hidden below the sandy dunes,
Along with the nightmares I have endured.
It is all a blurry, chaotic mess inside my mind,
Way down deep inside, unseen.
As I sit here, frozen in disbelief,
I wish there was something more to my flesh.
Only saturated loneliness stays here inside,
Drowning in my warped feelings of regret.
The emptiness is raping me from the inside,
Stripping my sanity with a merciless wind.

Bleeding it out of my veins with a coldness,
Until I cannot breathe here anymore.
I need a journey to take me away from this,
To pour meaning into my heart and fill my soul.
A stalling from the silence filled with my tears,
An actual role to play in this life of misery.
When things fade out slowly with a silent finality,
And numbness has taken over all that is me,
I have finally fallen overboard and let it take me,
And only saturated loneliness will remain.

Visiting You Here

I kneel upon the leaves with bare legs,
And feel the cold seep deep into my bones.
I welcome the slow, breeze around me;
It wraps me in familiarity.
I place my hand upon your stone,
And brush away the remnants of fall.
Seeing your name etched in the hardness
Sends me spiraling back in a silent rush.
Everything around me seems to liquefy,
Heavily veiled against my thoughts.
And so I feel your presence coursing
Through my veins, central to my heart.
After twelve years of visiting you here,
The smell of wet leaves and damp earth
Rearranges your conversant smell,
And chips away at my memories, piece by piece.
I speak aloud to you almost every day,
And hear your answers internally.
But I don't think I can visit anymore—
My capacity to remember, failing.
I need to keep you concealed within,
To protect what little remains of you.
And replacing you with a gravesite
Smothers me in endless pain and regret.

Taken Too Soon

I heard of your passing today,
And my heart broke for your family.
Their world must now be cloaked in gray,
A loss too heavy to ever fully mend.
I wish you had more days in this world,
Had accomplished all of your many dreams,
Watched your children grow into shiny pearls,
Grown old together, with your love by your side.
Memories of your smile fill my memories with a chill,
Saying my childhood nickname with a tease.
One of the sweetest souls has been killed,
A husband, a father, a brother, a son.
One of the most kind people I have met.
When we were kids, you always made me laugh,
Especially when my teen angst was a threat.
You worried for others before yourself, always.
I wish we had more time to share and sit.
I regret we never got together,
I can see us laughing and watching our kids,
Telling stories of our not-so-glory days.
The world has lost a kind man today,
A beautiful heart that never hardened,
One who cherished his family always,
And will miss his fortieth birthday.
Taken too soon and without warning,
You will be missed more than words can say.
The tragedy of It, so alarming,
That peace will be hard-earned for those you knew.
Fly on, my friend, and soar up high,
I know there will be more for you to do.
On a higher plane, God will keep you by His side,
To put a smile upon his face too.

Void

I do not understand why,
I make my life so hard.
I can never seem to stay happy,
Never wanted to be this marred.
My life will always be empty,
No matter what I complete.
Everything stays chaotic,
Within myself, I compete.
I have to find the one thing
Missing from my life,
To make it all feel better,
To let me feel alive.
The real void in my heart
Begins with my mama.
Her loss hit me harder
Than the loss of my violent father.
Having her taken was hell,
Like the loss of breathing,
The strangulation of dreams,
The ceasing of feeling.
And even though she's with me,
It really makes it harder.
I still want mom's advice,
But I cannot really go to her.

I guess I should move on now,
Should let my mourning go,
But how do I move on
When I don't know where to go?

Penny the Lioness

One day, you appeared with a fresh face,
A rescued body of long, fluffy fur and tail,
Making it apparent you are the Queen of the house,
Or bap, bap, bap! With your claws, you'd prevail.
A beautiful calico lioness,
Meant to be my sassy spirit animal.
You'd steal our hearts with your bitchy demeanor,
And make our whole world feel magical.
And we loved you as our baby,
Tried to teach you lessons like parents.
Eating was at four, but you made it clear, meowing
for hours,
That noon would have been your actual preference.
As the years passed and you have gotten older,
And lounging became your every-hour pace,
You still loved your treats of nip and cheese,
And made every piece of paper and basket your
place.

Eleven years we loved you with all we had,
Out of the estimated eighteen that you stayed.
But lately, I could tell your frail body was in pain,
By the way your eyes cut through me with a blade.
The decision was made of love and grief,
For the bold child I had once seen,
And it was an honor to be with you
As you crossed that rainbow bridge a Queen.
My eyes, this day, are raw and red,
To say I will miss you is not enough,
But I know I did what you needed me to,
And we are both made of tough stuff.
I will love your daughter until she joins you
On that rainbow bridge, where kitty's dreams come
true.
Everyone gains their golden wings,
And they are served as Queens and Kings!

PART TWO

Baggage I Carried

Escaping the Moment

I want to love, but cannot.
So many feelings, mostly buried.
What I want seems so unreal—
I need to hide from it all.
I can't believe what I've been through,
My young life, seemingly hellish daily.
The good never fully swallowing the bad,
The evil in me is always exposed.
People misunderstand my actions regularly,
Consideration seems out of reach.
I grab for love and respect,
But it laughs in my face.
I cannot hold on to what I need.
Little things try to fill the space,
But the gaping hole is only half-full.
My anger turns to instant rage.

Self-confidence has been taken,
Since I lost the one who gave it all.
I bring misery and depression,
It encases me with unhappiness.
Alcohol, drugs, whatever helps,
They make the pain leave me.
But when I wake with the light,
The grief tears twice as hard.
I need escape from all of this,
I need a way to get out.
I need something to deter,
I need to be free of this pain.

Walking Away

I walk away from you this time,
With a boundless ache inside.
It isn't in displeasure that we part,
But the wisdom that our lives follow different paths.
We love each other with open hearts,
But harm ourselves greatly by doing so.
I cannot grow while you suffocate,
And you won't soar high on the ground with me.
I wish the anger could flow through me,
Heating my bones with the fire of fury,
And bring me to the numbness and cold
That comes with the walls I have built for so long.
But instead, I feel an anguish so real,
A daily deep pit in my stomach,
Where something wonderful is lacking,
And a scar will remain red and puffy.

Deep Regret

As I ponder this life of mine,
I feel such immense regret—
Sorrow for those moments passed,
And the pain I can never forget.
Through the happiness I feel today,
I wish that I could move on,
But I have been so deeply scarred
That life cannot carry on.
Too late to try to make amends,
No way to alter the past,
No time to be a child again.
I must continue on this path,
And now I see the toll it takes,
As every year I grow older,
Trying to handle disappointment,
While everyone just seems colder.
I feel my failures so deeply,
And give myself all the blame.
I try to veer the present,
But it ever stays the same.

Lost

I feel like an empty hole has destroyed,
A warm eruption of bleakness has entered,
Damaged my heart in a repetitive flare,
And leaving me with the sense of bare numbness.
I cannot even feel all the pain thrown at me—
A wall surrounds it, protecting my sanity.
Slowly, reality leaks out in waves and spurts,
As I wait for the explosion of pure agony.
I am immobile and cold to the hard truths,
To a life that has altered from understanding,
Changing the rainbow from bright to dull,
Leaving the little bits of happiness lacking somehow.
Denial is a place I need to dwell in frequently;
It's hard, rough edges welcome me quickly.
And slowly, I eventually leave its grasp,
And a whine of loss can be heard inside my head.
I am tired and drained from this experience.
I cannot live the life strumming around me.
I exist only for everyone else I care about,
And save my dreams for my lonely bed.

Maze

A slow aching fills my heart,
With a silent bitterness.
I see the warmth of feeling,
Near the edge of my darkness.
But how am I to grasp
What I have never owned?
What has ever eluded,
What I have never known?
I reach out in the shadows,
Only to find more lies.
My angry tears reveal
The despair in my eyes.
The end of any trust,
The beginning of my rage,
Leaving me trapped inside,
As if my mind were a maze.

Most Days

Give, stolen, broken.
Take, mistake, heartbreak.
Irritated, violated, raped.
Regret, depressed, repressed.
Everything, something, nothing.
Mending, bending, ending.

Mothers Guilt

A simple yearning need to feel free,
For just one truly peaceful day— away,
From the weight of stress, of family,
And the clamor of what's "normal," and "healthy."
She cannot take in all of the pressure—
From the small, grinding downs and ups, the bumps,
To one great tragedy after another
The strength demanded to play a wife, a mother.
Daily taking what she can get from him,
And leaving the mistress the rest, the best?
The wife she is assumed to be grows dim,
Silent, and clinging to the rim, to him.
She needs to finally let him go to hell
But is she deeply in love— hard love, real love?
She struggles to pass through his grey spell
Vowing to never let him know how far she fell,
bespelled
A mother who loves entirely too deep
She loves them each greater than herself, her own
health
The smallest promise to them she cannot keep,
Will make her feel sick and somehow incomplete.
But where did the young pistol go;
A potentially powerful woman, humble?
Innocence somehow lost from sight, in flight,

The time to escape from it all so minimal
An immediate push back to real life, probable.
Marijuana has become her only relief
From all the darkness that rekindles her grief.
A gaping sea of wishes, of regrets,
And a future she hasn't yet dared to accept.
She cannot hold on to all that is gone,
Fighting memories she can't exhaust.
Clawing to build up her false outward song,
Hoping life won't thrust her where she does not belong.
The divine happiness she desperately seeks,
Cannot be filled with hidden lies, or blind compromise.
Nothing she is given can ever complete,
The eternal war within her—to compete.

Ignorance Turned Against Me

Almost doesn't hurt any less,
Because I walked away physically safe.
The pain claws at my heart just as deep,
The tears stream like blood down my face.
Dignity was stripped away that night,
Innocence lost in a man's need.
When "No!" dissolved into cries of fear,
Self-respect taken over by depression.
My ignorance turned against me,
Violently ripping at my flesh.
Fear chained me from fighting off,
My body and soul were viciously violated.
When he was done, I was released,
My first thoughts were of complete vengeance.
But then a call, warning of repeated affliction,
He remained my greatest fear always.
And he won with my silent pain,
My skin never felt uncontaminated again.
Shrouded and stashed away for ten years,
I now grieve for my forfeited childhood.

A New Life Drawn

Seventeen without a dream,
Haunted by a past she can't redeem.

Sex, drugs, and rock and roll,
Controlled the flow of her demons.

Dwelling on mistakes she couldn't take and
Hiding behind a mask she couldn't make work.

There was a need, a different person to be and

A control of the flow of her sea.

A little girl trapped in her own world
Unaware of the battles swirling around her

Brown hair and brown eyes make the perfect
disguise

For all the lies she buries inside.

A broken home, left all alone on her own,
with her rotten tone of true emptiness.

Her screaming soul beneath cries out "please,"

In a desperate tease to her heart.

Now, sitting at dawn, with a new life drawn,

She sifts through memories of days long gone.

Black and White

My heart internally bleeds like a waterfall
I cannot press hard enough to pause the flow,
And even if it halts for a while and seems okay,
The moment the pressure fades, blood spills over.
When I think on this, I feel a numbness sweep in
It protects me from the gaping inevitable wounds
So they never rush through this hard earned external layer.
But even this mask itself eventually starts to eat me alive.
I am not someone who has dealt with anything at all.
Withering in denial, alone in my room, for the last thirty years,
Feeling only what my heart can bear at that moment
Letting little pieces of chaos out just to ease my daily life,
I push my despair down to the dirt, beneath the roots,
And let it grow poisonous and spread with age and time.
It is only now, in this place that I'll realize the toll,

Yesterday viewed with only some sort of longing detachment,

My past is no longer my own, as I stare in fear from afar,

Set firmly in glue, screaming quietly to myself:

"How can life be so overwhelmingly complicated?

When all I have is this black and white stage to perform on?"

Taken Innocence

All advantages stripped away,
Leaving nothing left to believe.
Teen defiance became my enemy,
And no one stood for me.
A mere causality of the wants
Of a man without a spine.
My meager strength proved worthless
Icy flesh pressed against mine
Numbing pain ripped straight through me,
My taken innocence left bleeding.
Muscles tore and screamed for relief.
Coldness must replace feelings
As my only spine seized and I was raped.
With clear indignation and violence,
No more pondering my first time,
No more dreams of adolescence,
Left with nothing but bitter tears,
Always hopelessly jaded.
Never to mend the damage done
Ever lonely and faded.

Broken First Love

Lost in a haze of memories,
False love is all that is ever shown.
But faithlessness has shattered me,
And this, he must never know.
Drugs consume him day by day,
Trust was never his to keep.
Respect is not an option,
Apologies, he will not peep.
"Take some dirt to keep what you love,"
I hear this echo every day.
But that means burying myself
And I need to find another way.
He makes me feel so needed,
Then leaves me out of control,
But when he drains all my energy.
He then tries to play with my soul
I cannot live this lie with him,
And I know he is no good.
So why does it hurt so bad?
If I am doing what I should?

Forgotten Happiness

I am so lonely in this world of mine,
Forgotten happiness feels so hard to grasp.
Savoring my kids and my normal love of life
Just isn't enough for me anymore.
It's hard to let my past memories go—
The great ones linger, and stay awake,
Trying desperately to keep a little faith alive,
While the hard ones stay to conflict with my present.
I feel forever stranded in this fight,
Too stubborn to let them trample me,
But too weak to brush them away completely,
And so, they slowly eat me alive,
Always reflective yet never perceptive.

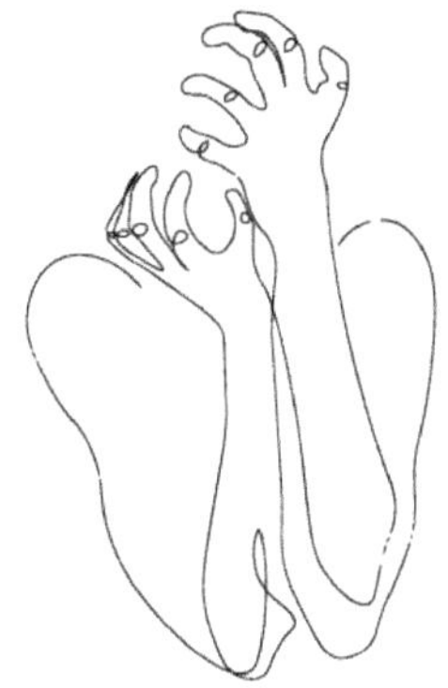

My Need to Scream

Pushed at, pulled, and broken,
There too much tension
Building up inside,
Catching me, stressing.
My anger's at its brink—
I'm ready to explode.
So many places it could go,
I'm ready to implode.
Every moment of worry,
Getting older by the second,
Can't seem to let it go.
Clear thoughts, I will beckon.
The hole inside me,
Cracks open wider,
Men after one thing:
"I'll just get inside her."
The life I am leading—
A single parent on my own,
Always begging for help,

Yet always ending up alone
Pressures from everywhere,
My strength is weakening fast.
Not sure what tomorrow holds,
Or if I'm up to the task.
But I'll try just one thing:
To end this whole mess,
Because I can't go on,
Can't live always stressed.
Can't keep wanting to
Hold it all deep inside—
I must let it out sometime,
Must confirm I'm still alive.
I'll scream!!!

Scarcely Sewn Fences

Moving slowly away from the door,
Your deception speaks volumes for you.
"I love you," you say, as if the words are made of truth,
When they are only born from selfish urgency.
"I'll make everything right, change what you want,
Only be with you forever, as I promised."
The words fall soundless to me these days—
I can only hear my bleeding heart breaking.
And now, after all of these years, you expect me
To repeat and reconsider your damaged life,
And make many more innumerable mistakes?.
It won't be me who is crushed this time.
You take every chance to hurt me with our memories—
A past filled with deceit and violation,
Souvenirs built on scarcely sewn fences,
Inevitably the strings, worn down and torn.
With every stab that you took at them
My love and faith in you was spoiled—
I gave you back your evasiveness,
And your selfish insecurities you can keep.
Think on this as you sit alone with your thoughts,
All the damage and abuse done in the name of love,
Let it fester like poison under your skin,
As it has infected mine for seven years.
I have no mercy for you in this life.
You create your own daily hell.
You will never know the peace I have,
Not an ounce of the serenity I have earned.
So, when your door falls off its hinge,
Don't knock on mine instead—
Cause no one here has pity for you.
We've all come and gone.

The Waters of the Past

All of my dark memories consume my mind and bury me.

Deep sorrow and regret take over, fracturing my very soul.

The pieces trapped in an immovable place inside my aching body,

Guiding me to relive all my most painful mistakes.

All I want to do is kill your lies and shove your ego down your throat.

How did you and your apathy break me in so many pieces?

Did you set out to destroy my insides and make me callous?

Well, it didn't work; I only came out stronger, and more resilient.

Yet there is a part of me that cannot move forward,

Unable to let go of a time when so many mistakes were made.

Holding me down under the waters of the past, struggling for air.

I need a positive change, that seems so elusive to me right now.

But I will inevitably begin a new life,
Free from your hate,

Absent of you all together.

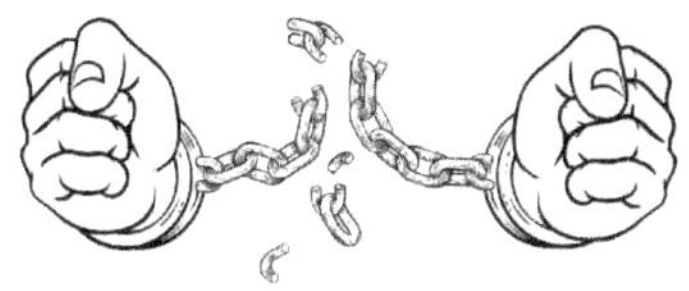

Irrefutable Life Truths

As a woman who once loved you always
In the midst of the pain you give
Lashing out with a hard oblivious whip
But an honest whip all the same.
I am slashing and tearing at all the internal
Devotion our offspring have offered you
While you have no intention, just dereliction,
to the suffering you cause
That I require you to claim.
The mere thought of a father deserving detention—
Eating their innocence within,
Slowly asserting each blow as a silent wound
To the depth of their souls.
They gave you the dedication that should
Only be given to a loving father,
But you have proven time and time again
That you just idly lack the tools.
The mere fact that you put them in
This position with your selfish behavior
Should make some kind of sense rush
To the self-inflated head of yours.
In their eyes, there would have been doubt and
anger
No matter what you actually did.

Your actions, in one moment, would have closed
those doors.
Each action we take has a reaction and
Can taint their lives in an undeniable way,
Altering the course of happiness that they
Ultimately begin in their pure youth—
That they deserve to keep.
We can all think back and remember the day
The last bit of our naivety seeped out,
A lot of times, only difficult pain and loneliness
Can emerge from irrefutable life truths.

Betraying Yourself

I feel your selfishly ignorant, and shallow behavior
Crash against the numb wall I've built for your
words.
Over and over, you throw the same nonsense my
way,
But I have long been over such basic truths about
you.
You're almost a child in the behavior you show,
In an adult's body, struggling to fit into someone's
mold.
Someone told you that fakeness and lies were living,
But you are stuck in a past full of teenage boys and
adrenaline.
Somehow you have passed two times their ages,
And yet your mentality stays exactly the same.
Dishonesty and the fake persona you've created
Will not see you through this life in any real form.
You will always be the loser that will never receive

The respect of a man whose childish behavior
creates only loss,
The father too selfish to try to be a good dad,
The person who everyone knows is not worth his
word.
Grow up and live the life you want to live with depth.
Realize now that life does not give you many
chances.
Understand that "daddy" only comes once in a
lifetime.
Don't take for granted what you refuse to
understand.

Anxiety

It's a restlessness that makes me move,
A tightening of my chest,
An ache in muscles that I haven't known,
And a pressure on my breath.
It comes on like a hurricane,
And flows from head to toe.
And when the noose will loosen up,
I never really know.

Mandy

The inviting sunny beach, with its sweet warmth,
As darkness falls slowly, a bonfire blazing in perfect time.
The breeze lifting the smells and sounds to her bedroom—
This is what I think of when Mandy comes to mind.
There was always room for being silly and laughing often,
An imaginative girl with brown braids in her hair, playing with her dolls.
Walking and dancing barefoot as much as possible,
And she loved her family and showed kindness to all.
I remember her singing Christmas songs in her first concert,
Her brown eyes bright, with a clip in her hair and a red Annie dress on.

Cherishing her animals, trains, and red Kool-Aid at Grandma's,

A simple child, trusting of everyone on any day, blessed.

But eventually, she was failed by her narrow surroundings,

First learning to stay quiet like a mouse to avoid the wrath,

And then bruised by more than the angry voices she lived with.

The innocence replaced with anger, moving forward on her path.

She was forced to carry that explosive rage alongside new anxiety,

The fear eating away at the innocence she once held close.

Deserving of love, but told over and over she was not.

She couldn't help but believe the lie more with every given dose,

And she believed she was nothing by the time she reached double digits.

Balancing to breathe while wading through waves of heartbreak and pain,

She was slowly asphyxiating with the expected smile on her young face,

And starving from the feelings of utter isolation and all-around disdain.

And now I think about that young girl over and over again.

I want to tell her she was never, even slightly, to blame,

That she is deserving of the love she so longed for,

And that her imagination and kindness have stayed the same.

That I am sorry she went through all of that, mostly on her own.

I am sorry she was conditioned not to believe in herself and be free.

And I am sorry I wasn't there to protect her and shield her innocence,

Because that little girl with braids in her hair— well, that was me.

And I want to say things would have been different if I had been there,

And I could have shown her what we would find the courage to be.

But my story was built upon that bruised base

And the fact is that I can't, and so for our childhood I grieve,

And miss her.

PART THREE

Love Finally Found

Beach

I miss the soft sway of sound,
Soothing water reaching for the still shore.
The smooth give of sand, setting a lazy pace,
A sedative to a day of stress and strain.

The First Time

In the bedroom, we wake,
With arms surrounding each other.
Our naked bodies embraced,
After our very first time together.
We wanted so long for this,
I thought we would surely melt,
Our bodies pressing firmly,
Expressing all emotions felt.
I turn to get up, but cannot—
My heart will not let me leave.
I love you deep in my soul,
But your thoughts, I cannot see.
I long for your touch once again,
I put my hand on your warm thigh,
I kiss you very softly,
We have a love I cannot deny.
As I give myself to you once more,
Your muscular body proves,
That you can learn what I need,
And your searching hands can soothe.

Afraid to Fall

(But Losing the Fight)
When you look at me,
I feel you from across the way,
The only one in the room—
I always want you to stay.
When you touch me,
All other senses fade,
My skin comes alive,
A re-connection made.
When you hold me,
I feel safe and loved,
Like any mistake I make,
We will rise above.
When you kiss me,
I cannot truly decide

How to show tender devotion,
Within a passionate glide.
When you make love to me,
I feel a joining of two,
That had been misplaced.
And now found each other true.
The feelings I have for you
Are scary and calming,
Crazy and beautiful,
And fierce and loving.

Wishing

I've been wishing for you
Praying on bended knee,
Someone who is real,
That person to be.
A true romantic,
An old loving soul,
A pure, funny man,
Lifestyles controlled.
You make my heart feel
Like it never has before—
Beautiful and full,
And really cared for.
You have no idea
How wonderful you are.
In my little world,
You are the star.
You're all I think about,
Given to me from above.
My romantic man,
I am falling in love.

Uncertainty

Confused beyond all reason or order,
The feelings are strong and overwhelming.
Naming them is a task I am not up for,
Reasoning them is an inability I can only own.
I feel a tunnel trying to surround my heart,
And the wall I have so carefully built,
That has protected me over the years,
Is crumbling day by day, brick by brick.
I feel you don't want my feeling to go this far,
That yours don't match the intensity of mine.
You say you feel the same way about me,
But no one has shared honesty with me in the past.
I don't know what you want or how you feel,
But I am falling off the edge suddenly,
To slam into the concrete and lose my heart,
And uncertainty is the least of my problems.

Losing Control

I delight in the way you look at me,
Putting your love deep in my heart and soul.
And over these years, one thing stayed true—
The way you help me lose all control.
As you stroke my skin so very gently,
I feel your intense love for me in your hands.
Every touch excites me all the more,
Needing to travel to all of your lands.
And when you please my wanton body,
You fulfill my every carnal desire.
Our bodies intertwining wildly,
Our moist fruition hotter than fire.
Your uniquely lustful affection for me,
And your blissful passion in life to explore,
Are all I will ever need or want from you,
And I love you for this and so much more.

Tremendously Eager

The way you look at me makes me want to melt into
a puddle.
Thoughts disappear, and only the senses open to you
remain.
I long for your touch and your laughter when you
leave,
And like a druggy without a fix, withdrawal takes
over.
I wear your shirt sometimes and won't take it off
Until your smell stops lingering, bringing me
memories.
I sit at times, deep in my head, with thoughts of you,
Trying to relive your kisses or hear your sweet
words.
You make me smile even when a bad day looms,
Encouraging my passion to create and dream of
more.
You give me such a different outlook on life at times
And gaze at me like there is no one else in the world.
My laughter is something different, only for you,
Something better and in tune with your kind soul.
I have no way to describe my vast feelings for you,
But they are new and enormously special to me.
You hit my life like a ton of bricks, with a quickness
Opening my wounded heart to begin healing and
closing
To satiate again with your affection and warmth.
I have never experienced so much, so fast, with
another.
We don't get to enjoy as much time as we would like,
But the moments we have are invaluable and
precious.
I don't know where our ride in life will take us,
But I am tremendously eager to find out together.

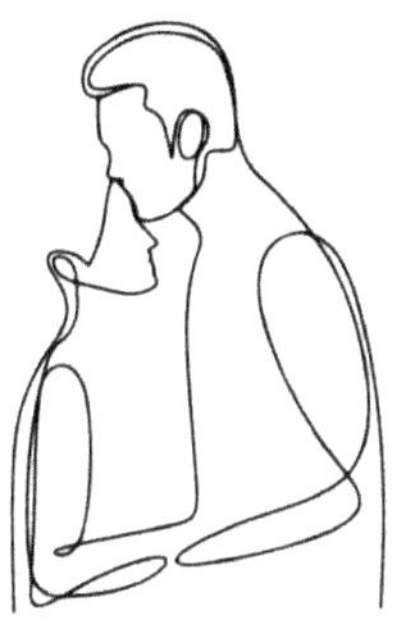

Sweetness

You look at me as a prize,
As someone worth your precious time,
A truly beautiful woman,
With a crazy, lovely side.
You make me feel so wanted
And soften my rough edges,
Give me hope for the future
With small meaningful pledges.
I cannot get over how quickly
Your warmth has crashed into me,
Eroding bricks from my well-built walls,
Without much chance to think or breathe.
Bringing me care and pleasure with ease,
A craving I have never felt before,
Happiness, I once thought undeserved,
And a fresh dream to explore.
My heartbeat changes for you,
My breathing relaxed yet deep,
A pulse I can feel under my skin,
A change I've so actively sought.

I miss you when I've just seen you,
Wish often for your hand in mine,
Your eyes lit up in laughter,
And every day, plenty of your time.

Toxic without you

I miss you like a thirst that is never quenched,
An ache that never subsides,
And a needed breath that just won't come—
Instead, it turns me colors that are beautiful,
Yet toxic without you.
I miss you like the trees miss the rain,
I need to drink from your hunger for life,
And cling to every drop I can consume,
In an effort to get me through
The long nights without you.
I feel an overwhelming need for you to be near,
To feel your breath on my neck,
To sense your lips seeking mine with eagerness,
Giving into the passion and life my body feels
When pressed up against yours.
It is a need I was not familiar with for years,
A perfect square that fits,
A lovely illusion brought into focus and strengthened,
And then taken from me when we are separated,
Only to be placed back in again.
I cannot even explain the happiness you bring with
you,
It is a scary, welcome overflow.

You have the ability to mend and break me,
To shine a new light on my ever-dark days,
Or make me feel the void without.
You listen to me when my thoughts are random,
Sifting through with me to find ease,
Calming me when anger or aggravation take sight,
And bringing sweet, fresh charm to my recently
broken life.
And your authenticity is a blessing to me without
disguise.

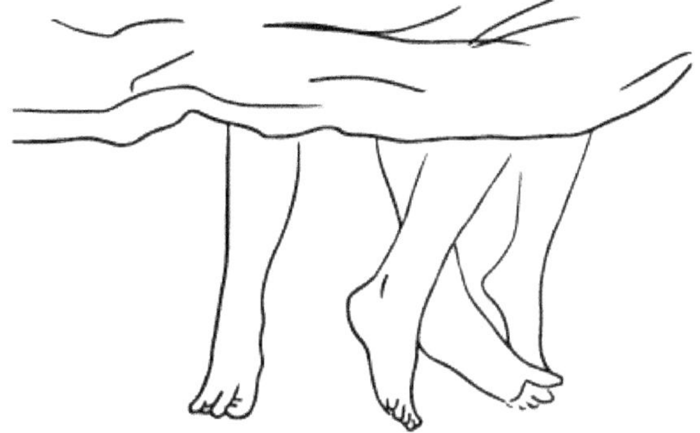

The Real Apex

She walks into the room, annoyed,
Her day has been taxing and long.
She changes into softer clothes
And turns to meet his smoldering gaze.
In an instant, her bad day melts away,
Everything becomes sensitive at once.
He takes her hand and leads her down
Onto the bed and into his arms.
He brushes her hair away from her face,
As his eyes smile at her with intense love—
An affectionate action that she longs for,
And her skin comes alive in reaction.
A desire for closeness takes over,
Clothes are shed in wildness and abandon,
Bodies explored in rapid, wanton touches.
Laughter and intensity consume the room
They fall into each other's arms once again
And surrender themselves to desire—
An ardor that cannot be challenged.

Hunger takes over to feed the ache.
Skin to skin, they melt into a rhythm
And find pleasure with one another.
Speaking fast words of lust and zeal,
United, a consuming climax is found.
After bodies relax and breathing restores,
The absolute apex is found—
The comfort of his arms around her,
Entwined, doing anything or nothing at all.
Love at its most perfectly passionate.

Holding Hands

Before this year of massive changes,
Deep love was a strange idea to me,
One I only really knew for my kids,
With a fierce, instinctual manner.
Every year, I kept moving forward,
Patching my wounds with the expected,
Struggling to grow and alter my course,
Without a partner to stand beside me.
After a doomed marriage between the young and
naive,
The immense loss of my main family bond,
And multiple health issues that continue—
All events which have molded my maturity
Into a capable, convincing adult,
With an ability to mime happiness,
Powerfully pushing through pain without regret,
Yet second-guessing every choice to be made.

And then a calm storm blew into my life,
With kind eyes and laughter that fills any room.
An untouched piece of my heart swelled,
And triggered a feeling foreign to me.
Holding hands with him is all I need,
Taking solace from his reassuring touch,
Giving him strong support in every way.
With a love built on trust and respect,
He makes me "more" in every way possible.
I am more beautiful in his presence,
More confident with him beside me,
And more in love than ever before.

Seven Years

I delight in the way you look at me,
Putting your love deep in my heart and soul.
And over these years, one thing stayed true—
The way you help me lose all control.
As you stroke my skin so very gently,
I feel your intense love for me in your hands.
Every touch exciting me all the more,
Needing to travel to all of your lands.
And when you please my wanton body,
You fulfill my every carnal desire.
Our bodies intertwining wildly,
Our love for each other hotter than fire.
Your uniquely lustful affection for me,
And your blissful passion in life to explore,
Are all I will ever need or want from you,
And I love you for this and so much more.

Side by Side

I thank my higher power every single day
That I met you exactly when I did.
If not, I would have missed out
And stayed so blind to what could have been.
I may have never really realized
What precisely I was missing—
The existence of a relationship like ours,
The care and love you give me daily.
Going shopping or on a date,
Road trips or silent conversations in public,
It doesn't matter what we do together—
We have fun in almost every situation.
With a look or a stroke of my hair,
There is nothing like the way you calm me
In many different predicaments,
Helping my health and other relationships.
And when you think I cannot see,
The way you look at me is beautiful.
The love in your kind and caring eyes
Fills my heart in a beat.

And when you make no comment
On the many times I silently cry,
It shows how well you would know that I would be
Thoroughly annoyed by the mention.
Within our bond, more than all else,
Is the pure peace that wraps around us
When you hold me tight in your arms—
Which is better than anything I could explain in
words.
We have laughed, cried, and fought,
But even when we fight and don't speak,
I know we are better united than apart
And will continue to grow into better partners.
I cannot wait to marry my best friend,
To proudly take your last name,
And most importantly, to continue
To spend the rest of our lives side by side.

Missed you

More than a few things surprised me while you were gone.
A two-week separation we had never experienced before.
I wouldn't let my mind wander about what you were doing,
Or long to tell you about everything I had done.
I lay in your spot once I settled every night,
I kept busy after work as much as I could.
I didn't fuss over the house until you were almost home.
I had to block you from my mind during the days.
I haven't taken as good of care of myself
As when you are here to remind me I matter.
I slept, but with a restlessness like I wasn't home,
Because my home was elsewhere.
I forgot who I was and who I aim to be without you.
I am glad you finally came home to me.
I missed you terribly.

PART FOUR

The Path Forward

In My Room with Headphones Blaring

In my room at sixteen behind a closed door,
I am ready to remove myself from my current hurt,
For a small frame of time where I feel in control,
Free to be myself within my own skin.
It is dark and tranquil on the outside,
But a heavy surge of sadness threatens inside.
My thoughts steadily twist me into knots,
Creating constant tidal waves of ebb and flow.
I try to slow the flow for a time,
Pausing the many thoughts playing in concert
With the stress I always put on myself
And the expectation I add from others I believe I've
let down.
Expressive music fills the room with an eruption,
While the cool night breeze brings summer scents
with it—
Beach sand, roses, and tulips enter the space,
And a calm wave of energy touches my soul.
Laying down, my thoughts go on a slow journey.
My senses are wrapped in scarred security,
Unaware that they fold me firmly in comfort.

I stay anchored to my body through only my breath.
In this moment, I am sheltered in my safe place.
I can be real, guarded behind my mental walls.
This place I have built feeds on my emotion
And briefly bandages my wounds through my senses.
In my room with headphones blaring,
Enveloping my very being through words of wisdom,
Purpose surfaces through my pain in this place,
And an obvious simplicity follows.
There is nothing like this altered atmosphere I
created—
I constructed it to cope with concerns as a teen,
To deal with the disappointment life can, and did,
bring,
And to shield me from the weight of my world.
But even this place has its faults and errors.
I learned to take my access for granted.
The physical place was seemingly insignificant.
As a child, I thought the world would hand me other
options,
But when I try to recreate this place of safety,
As the years push forward into middle age,
The missing sensations slay any chance I have.
The damaged bricks remain bare and unfilled.
More than twenty years have changed me in drastic
ways,
And the wall that remains is not built the same.
The place is different mentally and physically.
Even the music holds a different cause and clarity.
What is left is the life I have built for myself—
The detailed decisions I have made over decades,
The many mistakes that brought me value,
And the love I have surrounding me daily.
Still, I long for the crisp, clear energy
That naturally came from my home long ago.
The same place I wanted to run far from
Is now the place I long for with maturity.

Deep In Thought I Forgive Almost Everyone

So caught up in the uncertainty of the past,
I forget the present that anticipates my entrance.
Dwelling on all the little things that cannot be changed,
Instead of planning ahead to avoid the same errors.
I feel like I am outside of my body at times,
Stuck as an angry teen, dwelling on the demons to come—
Caged by the unhappiness that filled me long ago,
Unable to break free and embrace the life of right now.
Like an apple before the skin is peeled away:
From outward appearance, it seems mouth watering,
But when you can really taste deep inside the core,
You recognize it is all rotten and ruined from within.
And right or wrong, I cannot change the way I feel.
I have mourned the life I could have had too many times,
Pretending to move on, and forget my losses,
While my great pain thunders over my peaceful moments.
But my young children bring me soft illusions—
Glimpses of what a brave new morning is capable of bringing,
And present me with such wonderful possibilities
That were so obviously absent from the day before.
For a while, I can surrender myself to them,
And exist only in their pure, little open hearts,
So full of blind love and total optimism,
And a deep misconception of who I am today.
I have tried to forgive those those who caused me anguish,

Who raped me of the trust and vivacity that was
mine,
And left behind wounds that will never fully heal,
I continue to struggle with that formidable task.
Sometimes painting a soft smile on your saddened
soul,
Masking mental grief with the contentment that you
seek,
Can dull somber feelings your aching heart
conveys—
And dust off the real smile you have been hiding for
too long.

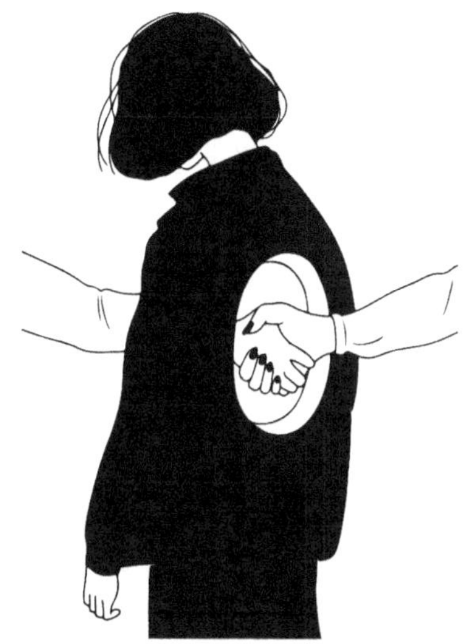

Health Insurance

The Drainer

The land of the free, the home of the sick,
With healthcare companies that think they are slick—
Thick with pricks, quick to save a buck,
And quicker to deny payment for anything asked of them.
While sitting behind their glass, masked from the public
With their green bias in hand and daft drafts of what is "basic."
Insurance companies let the unlicensed practice medicine,
Let them distract us, and repeatedly attack us,
Regarding our own health, and it is crisis of madness,

A blatant usurpation of a doctor's role as an expert.
But they divert your attention and pretend to care,
While asserting control, no matter who or what is left
bare.
All with the least exertion, chasing an extra dollar,
Throw out the scholar, bring in the white collar,
mislead
They can tell the caller that they need a smaller
waist size instead
Bring in the newly hired and hand them a typed-up
script,
Stripped of humanity and soaked with
condescension.
While skipping the actual problem and dripping with
deception,
Travel for a test that costs less, it's better they'll
guess.
Redo that painful procedure, and bless us with all
your small wealth,
Come on, play chess with what's left of your health,
Aggressively taunting quality of care as a goal,
doubtful.
When your policies are awful and audaciously not
useful,
For the benefit of the patient rings shameful.
Health Insurance: the drainer, the money-aimer,
The false-story painter, the small-hope claimer.
The obvious denial blamer, and
The insolent life-stainer.

Admissions of an Addict's Mother

As I lay my head down at night on my pillowcase,
I decide to believe you must still be okay—
Only because I haven't heard any differently.
As I speculate where your head lies recently.
The bed you choose to lay your head on at night
Shines a bright light on your current life.
Are the sheets you lay on dirty and stained?
Did you even find a bed to claim?
When I start my usual humdrum workday,
I wonder if you are even moveable yet today.
Were you up "partying" well past my sleepiness,
And giving yourself a false sense of happiness?
Did you anesthetize yourself before closing your
eyes?
Will they open to see the marvelous morning skies?
Will you ever be at peace again in this life, true?
Or will the internal war you wage spend and end
you?
When I eat my main meals during the day,

I ask myself if I think you have eaten today,
Or did the deliberate self-medication come first, the buy,
And the gut demand for food gets coerced into the high?
When I start my own daily self-tending
I ponder about your basic care and mending
Have you let yourself feel the truth of the dreams you desire?
Do you think of your health or what it will require to heal?
At what point did the little boy in my heart,
With the big, beautiful, curious eyes, start to depart?
When did the caring mind, once bigger than the world,
Become so angry and overwhelmed and let his life unfurl?
When did your incessantly regular motto meet
Your need to blame, lie, cheat, steal, and then repeat,
And include any routine with a numbing high involved?
My estimation, as your mom, is fourteen. But that's unsolved.
And a younger people pleaser is so pliable!
Being taught to spew words so deniable.
Handed the example of a "functional" addict,
By a dad whose life didn't seem chaotic to a boy
I know from my own addictions infecting my life,
Despite the advice so many tried, but I declined.
Alcohol, acid, cocaine, weed, and food.
These are what I pursued in excess, and it screwed me.
And I have learned firsthand, drugs that alter, are vicious
And the voice they bring,an enchanting malicious mistress at command.
Demanding absolute and all-consuming dedication,
And giving nothing but desperation for the next rush.

As your mom, I want to fix this for you in finality.
But my personal battle has quieted in totality
While yours is a roar waiting to be provoked,
At a decibel unfathomable and unreachable by most.
I want to give you the strength to fight,
By being a loud bright light, that you know will
support you in this life,
And reminding you of your nerve and self-worth,
And the abilities and possibilities ingrained in you
from birth.
Still, there is a part of me that wants to start to
scream
Over and over in an extreme bloodcurdling way.
To let the pain of watching your prolonged battle.
Unravel and surface but it's worthless, besting me as
well.
That part is the mom of that little boy, and she
doesn't understand,
She demands to know the truth of what has
happened to his joy!
She holds me accountable for every turn and twist,
She sobs madly at the once preventable reality with
clenched fists.
But I do realize that mistress is a deafening bitch,
Beckoning and nagging you until your bones hurt
and twist.
Exhausting and taunting your thoughts of dissent,
Until halting to yield is all you have left.
With sorrow, I realize I cannot fix this for you.
That is a resistant, bitter pill to mix and swallow.
That my son's mother cannot make all the noise
stop,
And hand him the peace he deserves but destroys
and avoids.
Yet if I succeed in saving you from your dire
ramifications,
It would only prolong your disease and slow your
revelations.

And that may not lead to much needed
conversations,
To aid in the level of life alterations that you need.
In fact, it is not my place to do this for you, we
know.
Something my own grown son can and should do on
his own, alone.
One decision would beat the boisterous bitch back,
Start the road to recovery and crack the mask.
It has to be your choice to seek assistance from
strangers with medical degrees.
Seize the chemical and ease the natural skeptical
concerns you have,flee.
It has to be your choice to dodge the obstacles and
make the hard decisions,
Come forward with admissions without omissions or
revisions.
To resist for a life of peace instead of imprisonment.
To cease the street life you are living in this moment.
To quit feeling like unwanted garbage all the time.
And to halt being a hostage in this life of carnage.
Ridding yourself of toxic influences who make you
feel boxed in, disable,
Those who enable for reasons of selfishness and
betrayal,
Facing the demons that made you hide inside the
numbness,
Stepping off the path you are on, and making the
changes required. Before you die.
IT IS UP TO YOU!!

We all have different struggles in life to climb.
Things in our path that can either destroy or design,
Your trial seems to start on a steeper scale
It will call for courage, but I know you can prevail,
It is in your hands as it has been all along,
We both need to face that fact head on
I am still the loudest cheerleader you've known,

But ultimately the play must be yours, and you're alone.
As for me, I have to be willing to let go of this obsession,
Not of my son, but the infection of his addiction.
Over him from afar as he continues to fight,
And look to changes that I can make in my own life.

From the Past

On this day, an obvious new chapter reveals,
Within the forest, damp and cool.
The leaves crunch on the path before me,
Absorbing my thoughts with their forward pace.
The dress brushes my legs like a kiss,
Hair traces my sagging shoulders
Hands grasp onto each other for calm
And instead, their strength turns my skin pale.
I hold a rose in my numb hands,
Reliving memories and faded desires.
Pedals caress my chest in the breeze,
The mist completing my trance-like gait.
A thorn punctures through my raw skin,
With a blast of angry recollections.
But I keep walking, never breaking stride,
And push toward a new dawn.
From the past, I progress with anticipation
My ignorance and youth dripping away,
Carrying my scars and hard-earned lessons,
To make it through the new trials ahead.

Progression in Pain

She went from another domestic violence victim,
So terrified of everything, she wet herself
Rather than leaving her room at night. *She was seven*.

To teenager seeking escape at a party,
Only to discover the cruelty of a man's desires—
A shower couldn't wash away the stain. *She was fourteen.*

Then partying instead of going to classes
And drinking became the main form of escape from her life
Still wanting everything she did not have and
suffering for the want. *She was seventeen.*

Next, she was a young mother working multiple jobs,
Blind to her morals and caught up in staying with her bad decisions
And drinking spiraled into drugs that took over. *She was twenty-one.*

By twenty-six, she had three children
And a second heart surgery planned—
And she thought she would lose her young life; Was it too late for her slow path to redemption?
But the surgery was a success, and her life started to change.
Mostly sober and desperate for help, she was struggling yet aware,
Of the pain she caused others and made for herself.
And that there were corrections that needed to be made,
She finally and completely rid herself of her worst decision.
She battled her demons for years.
And found her strength more every day. *She was thirty.*
She stopped focusing on the past and moved to the future.

She moved past the *silhouettes of sadness and self-doubt.*
She found a partner, instead of a tormentor.
She found purpose instead of just survival.
She found a better perspective than victim.
She found her power, inside of her pain.
And she finally set her baggage down.

Loving my Body

The changes that I see within
After more than four decades of time
Turn me sternly against myself,
In my own confused mind.
But when I look at others,
I see beauty in those lines—
Patience in their abused hands,
And in their eyes, an unbelievable shine.
So why am I kinder with others,
In judgement and in every day,
Putting myself in their shoes,
At both work and play?
I hold myself to a higher standard,
Is what I normally say to myself,
"I need to be close to perfection!"
My inner child and ego yell.
But that sets me up for failure—
A goal I could never attain.
It just leaves me stuck in the mud,
And in that vicious cycle I remain.
Chaos and disorder are both part of life;
And when they plan events, they aren't neat,
They leave internal messes to understand,

The destruction is achingly complete.
At times, time and healing is needed.
Scars and sags remain in their place—
War wounds and plenty of funny stories,
Memories that cannot be replaced.
And also, trauma lurking behind it all
Lessons learned with tears and grit, fought
Badges earned by sheer determination,
And yet, to those irrational thoughts,
I submit.
But acceptance of yourself is key—
To silence your insecurities.
And let the past stay where it belongs,
But this is not easy, this slow maturity
Embrace the lines of your body,
The chipped tooth with a story, curious
The lines in your hands from hard work, serious.
The scar from a traumatic experience,
The extra weight you can't keep carrying,
The eyes that struggle to see without glasses,
The wrinkles from all the smiles and frowns,
The way stairs turn your legs to molasses.
If you wish to close the door on your past,
Make your self-doubt be silent,
And open yourself up to happy changes,
While keeping your place in the present.
You cannot begin while holding negativity—
If you cling to it, it will sap your strength.
Start the war with a warped sense of self,
Before you can take the time to even think
Acceptance is the starting point of it all
The reality of the origin of your journey is important,
reference
Without it how do we know what challenges we have
already conquered?
And how to battle against the inherent internal
indifference?

Remember

When we are young and self-involved,
Before we really understand our roles or what we want,
We dwell on all that is not going our way,
And focus on the world we have created around ourselves.
But when age etches deeply in our skin,
Experience skews our once simple perspective.
And time seems to flood past like a wave,
We lose the innocence we need so desperately.
To get through the harsh ugly periods,
To really enjoy the beautiful easy occasions,
And to appreciate those rarely seen times,
That everything is harmonious and effortless.
It is too easy to surrender to the bore of everyday life,
To let the familiar humdrum take over for us,
And to forget those most essential to our lives.
At the past stages of life, we have been through,
Our personal symphony changes with knowledge.

All pain is seen from vastly differing objectivity,

Lessons are learned through incredibly distinct patterns,

And the capacity to withstand is our own, and no one else's.

Put the warped withered glass of decades down

And instead look at life as it is meant to be, a blessing

Remember to take a breath and be in the moment

For time is not something gifted to everyone in this life.

Song Writer

A face that inspires words of thought
Manor that brings a need to be retaught
A truth teller of the bluntest sort,
Giving reality like a daily report.
Speaking the part with a kind torture
In a soft room full of spirit and anger.
Permeating your skin without permission
But the worth of the speech puts you into
submission.
Words bring ideas of what is now,
And how it is possible to differ somehow.
No more will we allow robbing desire to change,
Them stepping far away and placing all the blame.
Or change becoming an elaborate illusion,
Leading to false confession and confusion.
You can't tell me what to stand for,
When my back aches and my hands are sore.
Anything worth having is hard to get
The wars of the past, we can never forget.
Live your life without fear or delusion,
Your words need to be your own soul's conclusion.

Significant and Immensely Stirring

(Ode to Korn)
Into the vast room, you progress,
Carefully taking it all in.
Thousands are there with you,
All waiting for the same thing.
Excitement intensifies with every step,
Placing yourself amongst them carefully.
The heat takes you over all at once,
Sweat and smoke permeate the air.
The stage lights decline softly,
Your heart accelerates smoothly.
Anticipation fills the room,
Complete stimulation is coming.
Your body wants to erupt
With passion and awakening.
It's a pure need to be this content—

Like an addict's quick fix seems healing.
Finally, the air leaves the room,
And a slow drum beat arrives.
Electricity flows through you,
And the crowd begins to sway.
As your eyes close with expectation,
You gradually depart from your body.
Inside your childhood bedroom, you go,
Sixteen with headphones blaring.
But before long, you come to recognize—
As you remember your physical body
It is much better to re-join the masses
And unite inside their vast motion.
Sharing this personal experience
With a mob full of strangers,
Saturated with great emotion
And unforeseen personal meaning.
The endless crowd robs you of air again,
And you give in to the crush of bodies.
With the press of skin against skin
Transfers their experience and excitement.
You finally feel full of purpose,
A sudden answer to it all—
Where you are part of something,
Something significant and immensely stirring.

A Laughter Orgasm

I want it,
So bad I can taste it,
My lips curving, my eyes shining, a smile filling up
my face
Until I feel some contentment.
So far from my grasp
It's happiness deleted, it's sound muted, its touch
too far away,
Totally taken from my memory.
The healing powers within,
Deep in my soul, down to my toes, and tightening
my muscles—
A good laughter orgasm.
Truly letting go of myself,
Giving up the fight, not caring what's right,
Clearing out my mind, pushing the past behind.
But it has eluded
For so long I can't breathe, can't let anything be,
Can't give in to living instead of just living to give.
A laugh comes with a smile—
A joke on myself, a silly act, a comic with no tact.
Nothing else like it,
No feeling quite the same, no one else to blame.
Why can't I laugh?
I want to hear my own voice filled with happiness
inside,
Instead of dark holes that no one knows,
And can never find, in this cave of mine.
If I had one wish, it would be to exist
With only laughter in my life—
Steadily keeping me alive,
Pushing air through my lungs, pushing blood through
my heart,
Keeping me miles apart from the stress that starts.
A laughter orgasm-

So good to taste but so hard to touch in this life of
too much.
An orgasm of laughter—
It will cure my soul fill in the hole and clean away my
sins
I want it, I need it, and until I feed it—
This hunger of mine—
I will feel incomplete, away from my feet,
ready to compete,
With my own soul out of control in an
alternate role.
A laughter orgasm.
It's all I need to be.

A Crazy Lovely Girl

She wakes up every day, planting a smile upon her face,

But deep inside, she hides her lies, slowly destroying her place.

She longs to reclaim all that was ripped from her long ago,

Cannot find the strength to enjoy her life without its woes.

Always living in her past, and building walls for men to find,

One moment of bliss never leaves her troubles far behind.

But her life has always been full of never-ending regret—

Starting the pretending with her father and his fury filled neglect.

An abused, "happy" child until she was ripped apart with her clothing,

A sullen, confused teen who wanted to leave this life with nothing.

When a content feeling would gradually come, washing over her need,

Her reaction would harden because she knew she didn't deserve to be.

A crazy, lovely girl with a continuously backwards thirty years,

A partier that was too busted too early to let loose without a beer.

She was never taught to shatter her defenses or alter her behavior;

She only knows how to sit in pure defiance and never waiver.

Hiding all of her fears from the small world that stitches her seams,

Wading her way through the storms that prevent growth of dreams.

Self-inflicted memories of pain seize the breath from her tired soul,

A stagnation that is so hard to live with and anger that is hard to control

In this moment, in this place, she cannot see beyond the past that is hers,

Feeding on the hate she was given and only seeing an emotion filled blur.

Judgment is handed out like candy in her repeatedly wounded heart,

Where she dwells now and the path to contentment seems too many miles apart.

Standing In a Courtyard at 3am

I am scared,
So very scared I cannot breath.
I know he's coming after me.
My ticking—
The ticking of my valve, too loud,
The surgery of which I am very proud.
Snapping twigs
Sound beneath his feet as he walks,
So very careful not to talk.
Senses on fire,
An omen of frightening doom—
What horrors will come from this loon?
Slickly lurking,
Concealing himself from all sight,
Hiding away in the deep, dark night.
Limbs shaking,
Afraid of what this could be,
Of all the things I cannot see.
Approaching—
I cannot let myself provoke
This crazy man, or he will choke
And end me.
Take my dignity with greed,
Then end my life for what I've seen.
The young man
Of whom I have been tense about,
He just made me loudly shout.
He's unstable,
A crazy dressed in a nice suit,
Determined to put me on mute.
A sweaty hand
Pressed against my trembling lips

Around my waist with a firm grip.
Quickly grabbing,
Pulling me to a different place,
Somewhere without any trace.
Ripping, tearing
At my clothes until they give—
Oh, please God, just let me live!
Inside of
My aching body as it fights,
Using every bit of my might.
Running fast,
Far away from this misery,
After I strike him forcibly.
Loudly screaming
As I run into the street,
Not really caring who I meet.
Finally done with
Another attack upon my soul—
A time a man took full control.
Not helpful,
A vague description, to say the least,
Of this man of whom I speak.
He disappeared
Never really seen by anyone—
I'll never know if he is done.
Left with a question—
Would he want to come back once more?
To finish what he started before?

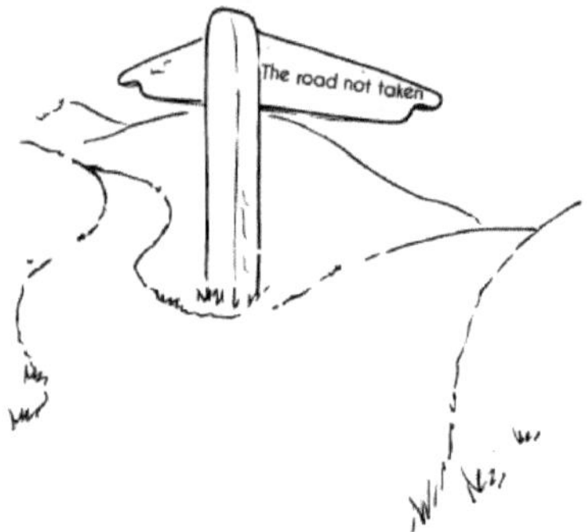

Changed My Outcome

A life lived in fear of disease,
Told I would not live past my third decade,
A heart that didn't want to cooperate,
And immunity that was frail, to say the least.
Abused by a mean-spirited man
With anger issues and cowardice,
Blamed for my body's reaction to the trauma
As the inherent differences in me began.
But the aftereffects lingered with doubts,
And I lost that man before I turned double digits.
His rage crept inside without my permission,
My father's weakness infected everyone in the house.
My poor decisions started causing me grief
And led to more detrimental choices,
Eventually spiraling completely out of control.
Drugs and alcohol became my relief.
Lost my mom as I became an adult,
And had my first heart surgery shortly after.

A stroke, a heart attack, and another surgery later,
And I could have stayed in the spiral of depression I built.
But though I didn't know what might come,
And they said my result was unknown,
I never felt that was my path,
And I knew I needed to change my outcome.
And so I worked hard, and one step at a time, I earned—
Making only the changes that would last:
Changing pain to determination and direction,
Grief to purpose, and trauma to lessons learned.
And I continue on this quest for me,
Put my faith in myself more than ever,
While keeping my feet grounded
And observing the change inside of me.

Unwelcome Traveler

No trust in a complete side of my body,
A grasp that will let go at its own will.
No reliability in the words I speak or write,
From thought to execution, they warp.
A painful gait that pretends to get better
From a monstrous procedure that saved me.
A singed, cloudy impression
Of another battle fought and barely won.
I cannot explain to you how a stroke feels
Or even how mine felt.
The sensory experience has been erased
Into a dull, fading nightmare—
I assume by the same wall I built long ago
For all immense, unimaginable pain.
I remember bits and pieces,
A scramble of sounds and sights and smells.
I was not afraid, as the idea of a stroke did not
connect—
Instead, oddly calm.
At some point, it occurred to me that I should be,
Which perplexed me.
And then, in a snap, I was strapped down
And forcefully flailing, or so I thought.
This pain I remember, though.
I can tell the effort was made to shield,
Yet I was meant to feel this pain
Over and over again as my reminder
That there was an immediate consequence
To my carelessness.
And then I was alone for hours at a time,
In a bed I could not move from,
With warring emotions
Flooding through me that I skillfully hid.
I'm alive, I can move, and I can think clearly—

But what lies ahead?
I cannot be let off this easy;
Easy is not my way of living.
Chances increase for another:
Stroke, seizures, dementia, etc.
And then, days later,
I am going through the motions
Of processing what happened.
I had a clot in my brain
That made my tissue think it was dead—
An unwelcome traveler
From my already damaged heart.
Then, when the clot was not completely gone,
A tube was fed
Through my body to my brain
To poke a hole in the clot.
This was a hell equal to
The two heart surgeries my body had already
endured.
And a tiredness came over me
In waves that made all others pale.
My thoughts rapidly changing from
A deep, humbling gratefulness for my life
And the time with my kids
To a dark, menacing shame of myself
That I could see from others.
From a deep, aching need to see my children
And to kiss their cheeks and say, "I love you"
To "Why keep me here rotting away in front of those
I love?"
I have always had a dark place
In my heart and head,
A place I keep the most damaging
Of my experiences away from today.
But this year's hurt alone has spilled over
The walls of that place.
And I feel a self-hatred and loathing

That is not so easily shaken off,
Which makes me feel ungrateful
For yet another miracle in my life—
Another year, month, day, minute
Past thirty; my original date of expiration.
I will move past this Cimmerian darkness
To the path I have been spared to walk,
To the purpose of this strange trip I am on.

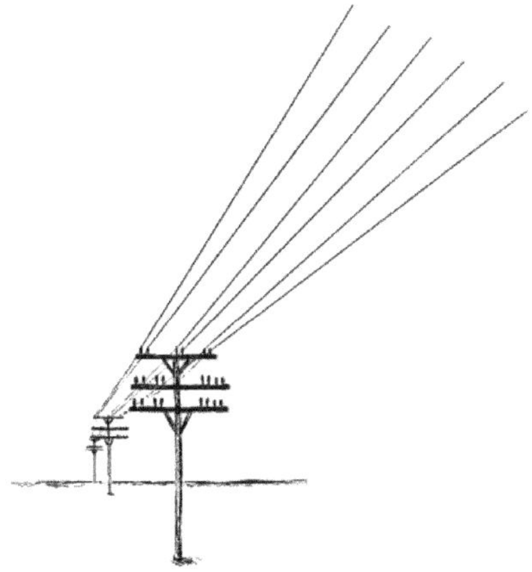

In the City of Lights

The Buffalo area is the place where I have grown,

For more than a century, as the City of Lights it has been known.

And even before that, a home to the Seneca Nation,

An area in the country well-known for giving donations.

Our Western New York history rich with diversity,

Despite our many seasons of challenge and adversity.

Here, a path for the Underground Railroad and the Erie Canal

Can be found, along with a historic park named LaSalle.

Home of Presidents Grover Cleveland and Millard Fillmore,

And the Central Terminal Train station, active during the first World War.

And in other wars, the battles near Fort Niagara, legendary,

As well as hosting the Pan-American Exposition, for us a cherry.

But we are also the City of Good Neighbors, and we make that plain,
With a history of welcoming immigrants again and again.
While steel and steam powered engines were our specialty,
A leader in grain, with the elevators still around to see.
We live near Scajaquada Creek, which GPS gets wrong,
But we are known country-wide as Buffalo Strong.
We truly celebrate Dyngus and Saint Patrick's Day,
And somewhere in our city, there is always a game to play.
If not at a game, we may be in a beach background,
Near Angola on the lake, where great hotdogs can be found.
We love our pop (not soda) and sponge candy,
Drive on the Thirty-Three and the One, Two and Nine Ninety.
Home to the Bisons, Sabres, Bandits, and Bills; wait, what's the score?
Baseball, hockey, lacrosse, football, and much more.
Experiencing our snow can be surprising with the lake effect,
Especially after a game, shouting "B-O-X, B-O-X!"
Or singing along to "Mister Brightside" with the Bills team,
While possibly eating a Beef on Weck and some ice cream.
Here we go through tables, and chicken wings were invented by chance.
We travel well and greet each other with "GO BILLS" walking past.
"Let's Go Buffalo" at every game we loudly avow,
But "Where else would you rather be than right here, right now?"

Unearthing Gratitude

Fearful of the possibility of losing—
My job, my loved one's life, my future,
My sanity in a world full of hate and injustice,
And of losing the optimism that runs through my veins.
Stressed about the unknown in virus form,
The safety precautions that sometimes change,
The contrast in conversations between world leaders,
The gapping divide that can be felt by everyone.
But so grateful for the breath in my body,
The love of my life, by my side everyday,
The voice I still have, to help change,
The health and wellness of those I cherish.
I cannot forget the power I have to move forward!

Collective Frustrations

Overwhelmed is not a long enough word
To describe the numbness I feel,
To explain how my thoughts go immediately dark,
To bring you to the 2021 world of the unreal.
What I need is a ban on outside reality,
To become a shut-in out of choice,
To bring my loved ones with me
And never look back at the noise.
But I cannot put myself in a bubble,
And I will not sit silent and indifferent.
I cannot ignore the injustice I see
While people die for being different.
Every day my ears bleed profusely
At more and more intolerance and hate,
Spreading like wildfire through this country
And the disgusting past is recreated.
My anxiety has me over the top
And paralyzed simultaneously.
I cannot comprehend how kindness does not lead

And how we do not deal with each other amicably.
Watching sons and daughters killed
On real-time videos that are imperative
To be the comparative in police encounters
And the following inevitable court narrative.
My anger and pain in witnessing these events
Does not compare to the despair of each family
As they lay their loved ones to rest too early
Because of someone's blatant disregard for
humanity.
But I feel it like a heaviness that follows
Every day, like an impossible weight on my chest,
Reminding me that change has to come for people to
live
Or everyone will continue to be stressed and
depressed.
Those of us who feel the collective frustration
And realize we are all directly affected at some level,
in some way,
Have a deep need to be a part of the actual
solution—
A resolution to this human persecution that no one
can gainsay.
Resist the urge to go numb with the obstruction of
progress,
And instead fight harder, make our voices louder,
guide.
Make historical truth heard across the generations,
And enact a deep impact that sweeps forward
worldwide.

Under the blankets

Starting the day on the cold, hard ground,
Covered in as many cloth layers as could be found.
The dirt where there is no deep rest—
Overnight, there is only being depressed and distressed
The night spent shivering through awake,
A highway of aches in a body that breaks.
A hidden existence from any uninvited guests,
In the body, an unrelenting stress is at rest.
Repeatedly questioning faith in this world today,
When one can work but can't keep the bills at bay.
Struggling to pay things off and create a base,
Where credit can aid in even landing a place.
During the day, others walk alongside their judgment, right past
The home made on the streets that won't last.
Most of them don't even give a thought,
But tell their friends it's a shame the politicians forgot.

The soldier, the teen, the addicts, all of the unlucky,
Little difference shown in the supposed land of the plenty.
The Veteran, after serving this country with no question,
The services that may actually be needed, never mentioned.
Coming home to help that is laced with judgment,
Living with wars raging inside of the brain, constant.
Or the teen locked out of the staples that should be,
Because of love, neglect, or parents that can't see.
A child lost in the decisions of the grown,
Or when stubborn important choices are blown.
When did we begin turning our backs on our own
And decide to turn away from anything resembling the unknown?
No matter the situation, treated like a ghost,
Denied compassion and forsaken by most.
This is a way of life all too common—
Under the blankets, they are shamed and forgotten.

Ode to the Indifferent Driver

To the driver who struggles to stop for sirens, what the heck?
Or slows to a maddening pace only to rubberneck,
Bent over the seat, looking elsewhere, rummaging,
Or follows too closely to react fast, menacing.
Someone who refuses to ever use a turn signal,
And the person swerving over lanes,sometimes triple.
Those who run red lights that are almost green,
And whose point is not safety but unbelievable speed.
Or enters the left lane void of ambition to move,
And to those who don't know how to alternate out of lots, improve.
When you crash, and that you will, marred,
Don't blame others, just look in the mirror, hard.

Decided Perception

Self-confidence is something to be worked on
vigorously,
And carved out of effort and faith in oneself,
deliberately.
There is a shift in people when they glimpse your
inner energy,
Even if they can't see your identity or where you are
mentally.
My directness has come from hard earned confidence
in myself,
Born from a lot of mental work and much needed
love of self,
I don't shun the consequences I bring upon myself,
I chose to own them instead of trying to put them on
the shelf.
I am very aware of my many personal weaknesses,
But they are not held up to the same light as my
greatnesses.
At last, I learned to put my baggage down and move
through my past,
But your response to my new healthier presentation
is in contrast.
Power is the capacity or ability to be influential
To others, using your credentials and vast potential.
But inside of that, there is a very hard lesson
In what others chose as their decided perception.

And there is an interpretation that comes automatic:
Men are just bosses and women are mostly
problematic
But while you feel my intensity is stuck up and
conceded,
Really, I am undefined and possibly undefeated.
Instead of praise or even neutrality, the judgement is
unrelenting,
Misrepresenting my words and suggesting I am
being condescending.
Just because you aren't in my head and cannot see
my vision,
You're somehow intimidated by the fact that I am
driven.
But while you are threatened by my obvious personal
ambition,
It's not my responsibility to aid in your lack of life
cognition.
It is very possible I may just not be your friend or
flavor;
Maybe look in the mirror, when you are looking for
bad behavior.
Work on yourself instead of openly judging others
There are many things about yourself you may
discover.
Deep in your belly lies a fire that is hibernating,
Until you find your plan and purpose, which can be
liberating.
But in the meantime, don't dare to take your shit out
on me.
My power does not rip you of yours, or your ability to
be free.

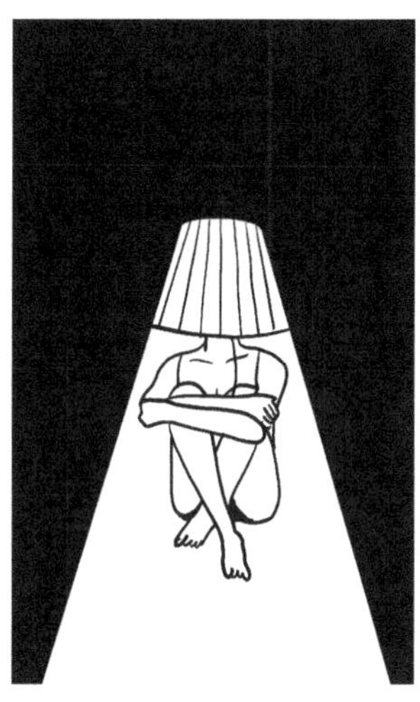

False incompetence weaponized

I am a second-class citizen in your eyes,
And with you, I see no firm path to compromise.
You build up that false power struggle we've had for
centuries,
And two thousand years doesn't dilute our
memories.
Project manager and modest subservient,
Sex slave and subject with a permanence.
"Hide the bleak life you live with outward cheer,"
For hundreds of years filled with stereotypes and
fear.
Punished for our inherent differences, and then
Burned from the influences of men with a pen.
"Don't let them find fear in what it is you say,

You may literally go up in flames one day."
Historically a scapegoat for the patriarchy,
Elitist male sexism— a familiar foe in society.
And it has been perpetuated by forced inequalities:
"What is your parentage? Never mind your qualities."
Demonized for using our specific intellect,
Quickly judged and shamed without respect.
While being hunted as a sexual object with beauty,
Men achieve, but women just do their duty.
The roles for women were detailed and dictated to them
By men with no care for her level of overwhelm.
Forever people pleasing while bearing the brunt,
With no strength in numbers to safely confront.
Raised this way for so many generations:
"Make sure you save face for your family reputation.
Worry about everyone else but yourself,
And put your feelings way up on the shelf."
Viewed as merely another property to command,
Eventually given possessions from a man's hand.
But they are misappropriated forcibly whenever he wants—
Our liberty, something used in chauvinistic bully taunts.
Throughout the years, we have had to rise up and rebel
While being perceived as small and gentile.
Pioneering and pushing for the right to be a person,
While men continued to make power assertions.
This became the norm because we were brainwashed,
And even after rights were granted, it hasn't been quashed.
Many still believe we need to stay in our own lane,
Because we perpetuate and allow that strain to remain.
And now, as we speak our truth with freedoms in hand,

Many of us still live life in a way that is less than.
The brunt of the labor with a reason to need him,
While he tightens his chains around our freedoms.
But that false incompetence has been weaponized,
While it drips from your tongue between the blatant
lies.
And emotional torture, by any other name,
Is a gun and a plan to forcibly place the blame.
Currently, too much feeling makes you
uncomfortable,
So, you go into great detail about how we are hard
to love.
I guess trying to make us small makes you feel large
While feeding your need to feel like you're in charge.
So while we speak our truth you "allow" all the words
But then cut them into little pieces so that "we will
learn"
Trying to meet your expectations is more than
exhausting
Especially with no thought from you on what it is
costing
Often happily planting your heavy feet on our backs
aptly
As long as you only have to do what you fancy
But no longer will we make our spirits small for you
Our voice will instead be loud and speak of truth
We are more than glad to be the villain in your story
To be rid of your debasement in future history
No longer will we help place bullies into power
But instead, will stand at the top of the watchtower
Making sure your jealousy and hate is kept at bay
And helping others access a way everyday
For this tightrope is too small for us to all meet
And we can all still feel the fires beneath our feet

Divided We Stand

After ripping the land from those who belonged to it, violently

They made sure those same people were thankful for the generosity

Rape the resources and devastate those you don't understand, betray

And so that example was put forward, and still stands tall today

Strip away our choices at an exhausting pace

While insisting "no one took them" to our bruised face

They fill their banks with potent power and blatant lies

Moral compromises hiding behind their status and ties

And push their fiscal agendas toward division

It won't matter later because the narrative will be rewritten

Fear of the unknown preserving their banknote religion

Just don't look while they touch the children and woman

Wearing fake platitudes and calling for your cultural destruction
While the masses drink the cult Kool-Aid and do absolutely nothing
Drifting dangerously past storms of aggression through the fog
The lies weighted down like their selfishness in the smog
It's easier to blame others than take responsibility
But it won't matter because they will wipe away our history
A broken culture that feeds the vultures that pray
Before our Veterans and vulnerable homeless may
It's their goal to create a false divide to stand on
While the death of the oceans and crops, rage on
And Mother Nature shows her wrath through frustration
But they continue seeking justification for their theft through degradation
Keep us pawns while starving us from useful education
And pit us against each other through the generations
Inhaling misinformation everywhere you step forward
While through automation critical thinking is slaughtered
Anesthetized to look away from shameful truths
Living comatose instead of asking what to do
But as they awaken the weightlessness recedes
And it is finally seen, how well and often they have been deceived
"Oh no! I let a liar change my mind"
But I do have morals and principals inside
So, what do I do and where do I begin?
How can I fight against corruption so chagrin?"
Open your eyes, and follow the money
If it doesn't make sense, investigate bluntly
Don't take anyone's word for anything, be frank

You will never be sure which poison they drank
Follow your gut to like minded people
And stay kind, fair and equal, it's lethal
To the hatred and greed keeping them motivated
Gather your core beliefs and be activated
This world is a slaughterhouse, and we are the meat
Together we fall as sheep, or divided we stand for
our rights on our feet

# The Crown of Thorns

When woman don't talk to each other
Or share their vast experience along with the failures
Give the advice they wish they had taken long ago
And pour random acts of kindness into strangers
And when we hold gags to our own mouths
Shut our eyes permanently to the new and scary
And plug our ears when others share diverse perspective
Generations of experience in pain and triumph are buried
And we pay that disservice forward for years to come
Through forced separation and the following of current norms
We let stigmas and other people's words, curb our instincts
And ultimately, allow others to place upon our heads, a Crown of Thorns
At first, we wear it proudly as if we earned each and every point

And have worked tirelessly to feel the weight of it
upon our heads
Enjoy the view from the wall we built of the way "it
just is" in the world
And cherish the anger that peers from beneath the
"normal" bloodshed
But really, the crown is steeped in defiant
dismissiveness
And placed on the back of massive unnecessary acts
of cruelty
To other women just struggling through the same
things we are
And shows ignorance and fear of what being a
woman can be
No longer should we live under the generations of
shadows
Doing what is expected of us when things are messy
In daily autopilot survival mode behind closed doors
Living with the heavy fears we carry, while quiet yet
dressy
Few men have felt the need to stand for us
throughout time
While we struggle for basic rights, medical care and
equality
Our votes have in fact counted less than a full
century
Even though in a general sense, we outlive men
historically
Rejecting what society deems "normal" is where
change lies
Through innovation, correction and choice we should
be leading
No more should only the men with money deem
what is acceptable
We need to take our strength and power, for it is our
bodies bleeding
Unquestioned acceptance is for self-love and your
intuition
Accountability and growth are necessities of a
healthy soul

Find peace within yourself instead of war with others
for belonging

And push the boundaries of what you think are your
only goals

And you may very well start a few fires along the
way

But common perspective and differing distinctive
voices

Move us past the ways we once deemed okay and
those words of poison

While opening avenues we couldn't see before with
vast choices

Question everything with your personal experience

Fight for what you deem worthy of your limited time
and energy

Learn about what is happening around you even
when it hurts

Listen to others and their differences, and gain
empathy

And find at least one passion for growth in your life

It will fill your soul with nourishment and love
without demands

Put down the Crown of Thorns we are forced to wear
by others

And straighten your Crown of Character crafted by
your own two hands

Unappreciated Blessings

Calm boring days with no to do list
The ability to travel without fear or debt
A slow morning before a rushed day
Friends who love you, entirely without judgment
The ability to choose a higher education
A restful day without the noise of guilt
The choice to ignore hateful behavior
The tranquility a day in nature can bring your soul
A pets undivided adoration
Shelter in a rainstorm with no end to be seen
A REM filled good night's sleep
The ability to hear your child's laughter
Clean air for our lungs to fill up with
Water that is clean, next to food that can be eaten
A body that cooperates with your brain's requests
Meaningful conversations with loved one's
A mind that is quiet when madness is near
Basic freedoms given to those not deemed "other"
People you love so much you physically feel it
Good health, especially in a poor house
The time that ticks away at slow and fast paces
The differences each of us bring to the table